Table of Contents

Introduction 3

   Benefits.. 3

   7-day meal plan 10

Recipe... 17

   Microwave Egg Caprese Breakfast Cups 17

   Mediterranean Mini Frittatas................................. 19

   Caprese Avocado Toast....................................... 21

   Mediterranean Breakfast Strata 24

   Greek Chicken Gyro Salad................................... 26

   Tuscan Tuna and White Bean Salad....................... 28

   Outrageous Herbacious Mediterranean Chickpea Salad 30

   Avocado Caprese Salad....................................... 31

   Citrus Shrimp and Avocado Salad.......................... 32

   Couscous with Sun-Dried Tomato and Feta............. 34

   Garlicky Swiss Chard and Chickpeas...................... 36

   Greek Salad with Avocado 37

   Whole Wheat Greek Pasta Salad 39

   Tomato and Hearts of Palm Salad 41

Quinoa Tabbouleh with Chickpeas Recipe 42

   Italian Chicken Wrap.. 44

   The BEST Chicken Piccata 45

Chopped Grilled Vegetable Bowl with Farro and Fresh Coast Retreat 47

Grilled Greek Chicken Kebabs 52

Shrimp Pasta with Roasted Red Peppers and Artichokes 55

Grilled Lemon Chicken Skewers 57

Greek Turkey Burgers with Tzatziki Sauce 59

Saucy Greek Baked Shrimp 62

Slow Cooker Chicken Cacciatore 64

Healthy Greek Yogurt Tzatziki Sauce 66

Mediterranean Quinoa Salad 67

Pesto and Garlic Shrimp Bruschetta Recipe 69

Pan-Seared Citrus Shrimp Recipe 71

Spicy Roasted Red Pepper Hummus 73

Greek Orzo Salad Recipe 75

Introduction

Scientists have identified blue zones across the world. These are locations where citizens live longer, healthier lives than in other regions. The reasons for these vary but often come down to diet. In Italy, Sardinia is the home to some of the oldest living denizens. The credit is mostly due to their adherence to a Mediterranean diet, which has become popular in other countries. Gardening for Mediterranean diets provides easy access to the fruits and vegetables necessary to follow this healthy lifestyle. Fruits and vegetables for a Mediterranean diet tend to prefer temperate conditions, but many are hardy. Items like olive oil, fresh fish, and fresh veggies are the highlights of the diet. While you can't grow a fish, you can plant foods that will enhance your Mediterranean lifestyle. Suggested foods for the Mediterranean diet garden are: Olives Cucumbers Celery Artichokes Tomatoes Figs Beans Dates Citrus Grapes Peppers Squash Mint Thyme.

Benefits

The Mediterranean Diet May Help Reduce Your Risk for Heart Disease

Numerous studies suggest the Mediterranean diet is good for your ticker, noted a meta-analysis published in November 2015 in the journal Critical Reviews in Food Science and Nutrition. Perhaps the most convincing evidence comes from a randomized clinical trial published in April 2013 in the New England Journal of Medicine, known as the PREDIMED study. For about five years, authors followed 7,000 women and men in Spain who had type 2 diabetes or a high risk for cardiovascular disease. Those who ate a calorie-unrestricted Mediterranean diet with extra-virgin olive oil or nuts had a 30 percent lower risk of heart events. Researchers didn't advise participants on exercise. The study authors reanalyzed the data at a later point to address a widely criticized flaw in the randomization protocol, and reported similar results in June 2018 in the New England Journal of Medicine. "That is probably the biggest scientific evidence to say that a Mediterranean diet is healthful, in terms of reducing the risk of cardiovascular disease," Carson says.

Eating a Mediterranean Diet May Reduce Women's Risk for Stroke

We already know from the PREDIMED study that eating in a Mediterranean fashion can help lower the risk of cardiovascular disease in some people. Well, the diet may also help reduce stroke risk in women, though researchers didn't observe the same results in men, according to a cohort study published in September 2018 in the journal Stroke. Researchers looked at a predominantly white group of 23,232 men and women ages 40 to 77 who lived in the United Kingdom. The more closely a woman followed a Mediterranean diet, the lower her risk of having a stroke. However, researchers didn't see statistically significant results in men. Most notably, in women who were at high risk of having a stroke, following the diet reduced their chances of this health event by 20 percent. Study authors don't know the reason for the difference, but they hypothesize that different types of strokes in men and women may play a role. A good next step toward understanding the reasons behind the differences would be a clinical trial, Carson says.

A Mediterranean Diet May Prevent Cognitive Decline and Alzheimer's Disease

As a heart-healthy diet, the Mediterranean eating pattern may also help to reduce a decline in your memory and thinking skills with age. "The brain is a very hungry organ. To supply all of those nutrients and oxygen [that it needs], you have to have a rich blood supply. So, people who are having any problems with their vascular health their blood vessels are really at increased risk for developing problems with their brain, and then that frequently will present itself as cognitive decline," says Keith Fargo, PhD, director of scientific programs and outreach for the Alzheimer's Association.

The Mediterranean Diet May Help With Weight Loss and Maintenance

Likely due to its focus on whole, fresh foods, the Mediterranean diet may help you lose weight in a safe and sustainable way, but if you're looking for fast results, you may be better off with a different diet plan. As mentioned, in its 2019 rankings, U.S. News & World Report rated the Mediterranean diet as No. 1 in its Best Diets Overall category, yet the diet tied with several other plans for the 17th position among the website's Best Weight Loss Diets.

Over a five-year period, eating a calorie-unrestricted Mediterranean diet high in unsaturated vegetable fat led to slightly more weight loss and added less to participants' waist circumferences than a low-fat diet, according to an analysis of the Spanish PREDIMED trial data that was published in August 2016 in the journal The Lancet: Diabetes and Endocrinology. Particularly, people who added extra-virgin olive oil to their diets lost the most weight 0.88 kilograms (kg), or 1.9 pounds (lbs) on average. Those who added nuts lost 0.4 kg on average (0.88 lbs), and those in the control group who ate a low-fat diet lost 0.6 kg (1.3 lbs). Once you add calorie restriction, the Mediterranean diet may show more dramatic results, though not necessarily beating out another popular diet approach. In a two-year randomized, clinical trial, 322 moderately obese middle-aged participants in Israel, who were mostly men, followed one of three diets: a calorie-restricted low-fat diet, a calorie-restricted Mediterranean diet, and a calorie-unrestricted low-carb diet.

Eating a Mediterranean Diet May Help Stave Off and Manage Type 2 Diabetes

For type 2 diabetes management and possible prevention, a Mediterranean diet may be the way to go. Using participants from the PREDIMED study, researchers randomized a subgroup of 418 people ages 55 to 80 without diabetes and followed up with them after four years to see if they had developed the disease. The results were published in the journal Diabetes Care. Those participants who followed the Mediterranean diet, whether supplementing with olive oil or nuts, had a 52 percent lower risk for type 2 diabetes during the four year follow-up, and they didn't necessarily lose weight or exercise more. Furthermore, a meta-analysis of 20 randomized clinical trials published in January 2013 in the American Journal of Clinical Nutrition found that the Mediterranean diet improved blood sugar control more than low-carbohydrate, low-glycemic index, and high-protein diets, in those managing type 2 diabetes. This finding suggests that a Mediterranean diet may be an effective way to help ward off type 2 diabetes–related health complications.

Are Foods in the Mediterranean Diet Protective Against Cancer

Indeed, a Mediterranean diet meal plan may help prevent certain types of cancer. A meta-analysis and review of 83 studies published in October 2017 in the journal Nutrients suggested the Mediterranean diet may help reduce the risk of cancers such as breast cancer and colorectal cancer, and help prevent cancer-related death. "These observed beneficial effects are mainly driven by higher intakes of fruits, vegetables, and whole grains," the authors wrote. A separate study, published in October 2015 in the journal JAMA Internal Medicine and based on PREDIMED data, found that women who ate a Mediterranean diet supplemented with extra-virgin olive oil had a 62 percent lower risk of breast cancer than those in the control group that ate a low-fat diet.

Eating Foods in a Mediterranean Diet May Help Ease Depression

The Mediterranean way of eating is linked to lower incidence of depression, according to an analysis of 41 observational studies published in September 2018 in the journal Molecular Psychiatry. Analysis of pooled data from four longitudinal studies revealed that the diet was associated with a 33 percent reduced risk of depression, compared with following a "pro-inflammatory diet" (richer in processed meats, sugar, and trans fats) that is more typical of a standard American diet. While the study didn't reveal why a Mediterranean diet lowered depression risk, the study authors wrote that their results may be a launching point to develop and study diet-based interventions for depression.

7-day meal plan

Here is an example of a 7-day Mediterranean diet meal plan:

Day 1

One breakfast option is greek yogurt with blueberries and walnuts.

Breakfast

• one pan-fried egg

• whole-wheat toast

• grilled tomatoes

For additional calories, add another egg or some sliced avocado to the toast.

Lunch

• 2 cups of mixed salad greens with cherry tomatoes and olives on top and a dressing of olive oil and vinegar

• whole-grain pita bread

• 2 ounces (oz) of hummus

Dinner

• Whole-grain pizza with tomato sauce, grilled vegetables, and low-fat cheese as toppings

• For added calories, add some shredded chicken, ham, tuna, or pine nuts to the pizza.

Day 2

Breakfast

• 1 cup of Greek yogurt

• Half a cup of fruits, such as blueberries, raspberries, or chopped nectarines

For additional calories, add 1–2 oz of almonds or walnuts.

Lunch

• Whole-grain sandwich with grilled vegetables, such as eggplant, zucchini, bell pepper, and onion

• To increase the calorie content, spread hummus or avocado on the bread before adding the fillings.

Dinner

• One portion of baked cod or salmon with garlic and black pepper to add flavor

• One roasted potato with olive oil and chives

Day 3

Breakfast

• 1 cup of whole-grain oats with cinnamon, dates, and honey

• Top with low-sugar fruits, such as raspberries

• 1 oz of shredded almonds (optional)

Lunch

• Boiled white beans with spices, such as laurel, garlic, and cumin

• 1 cup of arugula with an olive oil dressing and toppings of tomato, cucumber, and feta cheese

Dinner

• one-half of a cup of whole-grain pasta with tomato sauce, olive oil, and grilled vegetables

• 1 tablespoon of Parmesan cheese

Day 4

Breakfast

• Two-egg scramble with bell peppers, onions, and tomatoes

• Top with 1 oz of queso fresco or one-quarter of an avocado

Lunch

• Roasted anchovies in olive oil on whole-grain toast with a sprinkling of lemon juice

• A warm salad comprising 2 cups of steamed kale and tomatoes

Dinner

• 2 cups of steamed spinach with a sprinkling of lemon juice and herbs

• One boiled artichoke with olive oil, garlic powder, and salt

• Add another artichoke for a hearty, filling meal.

Day 5

Breakfast

• 1 cup of Greek yogurt with cinnamon and honey on top

• Mix in a chopped apple and shredded almonds

Lunch

• 1 cup of quinoa with bell peppers, sun-dried tomatoes, and olives

• Roasted garbanzo beans with oregano and thyme

• Top with feta cheese crumbles or avocado (optional)

Dinner

• 2 cups of steamed kale with tomato, cucumber, olives, lemon juice, and Parmesan cheese

• A portion of grilled sardines with a slice of lemon

Day 6

Breakfast

• Two slices of whole-grain toast with soft cheese, such as ricotta, queso fresco, or goat cheese

• Add chopped blueberries or figs for sweetness

Lunch

• 2 cups of mixed greens with tomato and cucumber

• A small portion of roasted chicken with a sprinkling of olive oil and lemon juice

Dinner

• Oven-roasted vegetables, such as:

• Artichoke

• Carrot

• Zucchini

• Eggplant

• Sweet potato

• Tomato

• Toss in olive oil and heavy herbs before roasting

• 1 cup of whole-grain couscous

Day 7

Breakfast

• Whole-grain oats with cinnamon, dates, and maple syrup

• Top with low-sugar fruits, such as raspberries or blackberries

Lunch

• Stewed zucchini, yellow squash, onion, and potato in a tomato and herb sauce

Dinner

• 2 cups of greens, such as arugula or spinach, with tomato, olives, and olive oil

• A small portion of white fish

• Leftover vegetable stew from lunch

Recipe

Microwave Egg Caprese Breakfast Cups

Just a spoonful of homemade pesto sauce adds plenty of flavor to these microwave eggs. Cooking time will vary depending on if you cook one or two eggs in the ramekin and how many ramekins you cook at once. And remember, cooking time will vary depending on the wattage of your microwave.

Ingredients

• 2 slices thinly sliced ham

• Shredded mozzarella or provolone or a mix of the two

• 2 eggs

• Basil pesto sauce

• Cherry tomatoes cut in half

• Kosher salt and freshly ground black pepper

• Fresh basil leaves if desired

Instructions

• Layer the slices of ham on the bottom and up the sides of a ramekin or small bowl pressing into the creases and ruffling the edges then sprinkle with the cheese.

• Crack the eggs into the ramekins and add a dollop of pesto over the eggs with a few cherry tomato halves and season with kosher salt and freshly ground black pepper.

• Place in the microwave and cover with a microwave plate cover and cook on high for 1 minute and 30 seconds or until the whites are set, adding additional 20 second bursts if needed. All microwaves will cook differently so play around with the amount of time. If cooking more than one set of eggs at a time allow for more cooking time as well. Garnish with fresh basil leaves and more kosher salt and black pepper if desired.

Mediterranean Mini Frittatas

Ingredients

• 6 large eggs

• 1/4 cup milk or half and half

• Kosher salt and freshly ground black pepper

• ¼ cup artichokes in oil drained and thinly sliced

• ⅓ cup pitted kalamata olives drained and quartered

• ¼ cup bottled sweet red peppers drained and chopped

• ½ cup sun-dried tomatoes in oil drained and chopped

• ¼ asiago cheese shredded

• ¼ feta cheese crumbled

• ¼ cup Italian flat leaf parsley chopped

Instructions

• Preheat the oven to 375 degrees F.

• Spray 2 mini muffin tins (with 12 cups each) with cooking spray. (I use this mini muffin tin

• Put eggs and milk, or half and half, in a blender and mix for 1-2 minutes.

• Fill each muffin tin ¾ full with the egg mixture.

• If using marinated or packaged flavorings, drain the oil from the vegetables before chopping. Evenly distribute the artichoke slices, kalamata olives, red peppers, sun dried tomatoes and asiago cheese among the muffin tins. Fill the tins to the top with more egg mixture then sprinkle with feta and parsley.

• Bake until the egg is set, about 10-12 minutes. The eggs will deflate somewhat once removed from the oven and as they cool.

• Run a knife around the edges of the frittatas to loosen them from the muffin cups. Serve immediately or at room temperature.

Recipe Notes

*note: To save in prep and rather than buying full size bottled ingredients, I used 1 package DeLallo Sharp Salad Savor Toppings and 1 package DeLallo Zesty Salad Savor

Toppings (which equals the amount of ingredients listed above) for all of the flavor additions to the egg base.

Caprese Avocado Toast

Cottage cheese subs in for mozzarella in this healthy avocado toast perfect for a favorite breakfast, lunch and snack.

Ingredients

- 1 slice whole-wheat toast

- 1-2 teaspoons flaxseed oil

- 1/2 avocado , peeled and sliced or mashed

- 1/3 cup low-fat cottage cheese

- 1 small tomato (I like campari tomatoes)

- Basil leaves , for garnish

- Flaked sea salt I like this one

Instructions

- Toast the bread and drizzle with flaxseed oil.

- Layer with the avocado, cottage cheese and tomato.

• Garnish with basil leaves and flaked sea salt and drizzle with a little more flaxseed oil if desired.

Mushroom and Asparagus Frittata with Goat Cheese

Frittatas are usually shared, but this two-egg, single-serving asparagus frittata recipe is the perfect way to enjoy a healthy breakfast idea for one.

Ingredients

• 2 eggs

• 1 teaspoon water (or milk)

• pinch of kosher salt

• 1 tablespoon butter (or Cooking spray)

• 3 brown mushrooms , sliced

• 5 asparagus spears , trimmed and cut into 1/2-inch pieces

• 1 tablespoon chopped green onion

• 2 tablespoons goat cheese

Instructions

• Preheat the oven or toaster oven to broil.

• Spray a 7- to 8-inch non-stick fry pan with cooking spray and warm on medium heat. Add the sliced mushrooms and cook for 2-3 minutes, turning once or twice. Add the asparagus and cook for 1-2 minutes more.

• Whisk the eggs in a bowl with 1 teaspoon water and a pinch of kosher salt until light and frothy, then pour into the mushroom and spinach mixture. Sprinkle with the green onion and the goat cheese.

• Cook the eggs undisturbed until the edges begin to pull away from the edge of the pan and begin to set. Gently lift the edges of the egg whites and tilt the pan so the uncooked egg runs under the cooked part and cook for another minute or so.

• Transfer the fry pan to the oven and broil for 2-3 minutes or until the eggs have puffed and have cooked through.

• Remove from the oven and sprinkle with more goat cheese if desired. Cut into wedges and serve warm or at room temperature.

Recipe Notes

This easy frittata serves one, but can easily stretch for two by adding a side salad or bowl of berries or fruit.

I suggest using water and cooking spray in the recipe to keep the recipe if you're looking to keep things on the lower fat side.

Mediterranean Breakfast Strata

Ingredients

• 3 tablespoons butter

• 2 cloves garlic minced

• 2 shallots minced

• 1 cup button mushrooms sliced

• 1 teaspoon dried marjoram leaves

• 6 cups white bread cut into 1/2 inch chunks

• 1/2 cup artichoke hearts cut into 1/8ths

• 1/4 cup kalamata olives quartered

• 1/4 cup marinated sun dried tomatoes slivered

• 1/4 cup shredded Parmesan cheese plus additional for topping

• 4 ounces or 1 cup Ciliegine Fresh Mozzarella cheese balls halved

• 6 eggs

• 1 1/2 cups half and half

• 1/4 cup basil leaves slivered

• Kosher salt

Instructions

• Melt 1 tablespoon butter. For individual stratas, brush insides of four 1-cup baking dishes. If serving family style, brush inside of 2-quart baking dish.

• Preheat oven to 325°F.

• In large skillet over medium heat, melt remaining 2 tablespoons butter. Add garlic and shallot; sauté for 2 minutes. Add mushrooms and marjoram and cook for another 4 minutes. Remove from heat and place mushroom mixture in large bowl with bread chunks, artichoke hearts, kalamata olives, sun dried tomatoes, Parmesan and Fresh Mozzarella and stir to mix. Season lightly with kosher salt. Fill baking dishes evenly with the bread mixture.

• In 4-cup liquid measuring cup, mix eggs with half and half and pour 1 cup of egg mixture evenly over bread in each dish. Garnish with basil and more Parmesan.

• Place baking dishes on a baking sheet and bake for 50 minutes or until eggs have set. Remove from oven and let rest 5 minutes before serving.

Greek Chicken Gyro Salad

I use my Greek Marinated Chicken Breast to maximize my favorite Mediterranean flavors, but you can always use shredded rotisserie chicken if time is an issue.

Servings 2 salads

Ingredients

• 6 cups chopped romaine lettuce

• 1 8- ounce Greek Marinated Chicken Breast sliced or chopped

• 1 15- ounce can garbanzo beans drained

• 1 cup cherry tomatoes sliced

• 1 cup sliced cucumber

• 1/2 avocado chopped

• 1/4 cup sliced kalamata olives

• 1/4 cup sliced red onion

• 2 pita bread pockets

• Canola oil spray

• Paprika

• 1/4 cup extra virgin olive oil

• 1/4 cup red wine vinegar

• 1 clove garlic peeled and minced

• 2 teaspoons oregano

• 1 teaspoon sugar

• 1/2 teaspoon each of kosher salt and freshly ground black pepper

• Homemade Tzatziki sauce for drizzling

Instructions

• Add the lettuce to a large serving bowl and top with the sliced chicken, garbanzo beans, tomatoes, cucumber, avocado, olives and red onion.

• Cut the pita breads into triangles and spray with canola oil. Sprinkle with paprika and toast until golden. Sprinkle with kosher salt.

• To make the dressing add the olive oil, red wine vinegar, garlic, oregano, sugar and salt and pepper to a small canning jar. Top with the lid and shake well until blended and emulsified. Season with more sugar and salt and pepper to taste.

• Drizzle the dressing over the salad and toss to taste. Drizzle with the tzatziki as desired.

Tuscan Tuna and White Bean Salad

This no-mayo tuna salad is dressed with a simple drizzle of olive oil and fresh lemon juice. For my salads, I prefer an olive oil with a fruity instead of grassy taste.

Ingredients

• 4 cups arugula (or spinach or other favorite lettuce)

• 15 ounces cannellini beans , rinsed and drained (or Great Northern beans)

• 5 ounces white albacore tuna packed in water , drained

• 1/2 cup cherry tomatoes , halved

• 1/4 cup sliced olives (green, Kalamata, or your favorite variety)

• Thinly sliced red onion

• 2 tablespoons extra virgin olive oil

• 1/2 lemon

• 1/4 cup crumbled feta cheese

• Kosher salt and freshly ground black pepper

Instructions

• In a large bowl or two smaller bowls, combine the arugula, white beans, tuna, tomatoes, olives and and red onion.

• Drizzle with the olive oil and the juice from the lemon. Toss to combine.

• Top with crumbled feta cheese and season to taste with kosher salt and black pepper.

Outrageous Herbacious Mediterranean Chickpea Salad
This easy Mediterranean chickpea salad is infused with flavor thanks to a heaping helping of fresh herbs and a garlicky lemon dressing.

Ingredients

• 30 ounces chickpeas (garbanzo beans) , rinsed and drained (or 3 cups cooked chickpeas)

• 1 medium red bell pepper , chopped

• 1 1/2 cups chopped fresh flat-leaf parsley , about 1 bunch

• 1/2 cup chopped red onion

• 1/2 cup chopped celery plus leaves , about 2 ribs

• 3 tablespoons extra virgin olive oil

• 3 tablespoons lemon juice (from 1 to 1 1/2 lemons)

• 2 cloves garlic , pressed or minced

• 1/2 teaspoon kosher salt

• 1/2 teaspoon freshly ground black pepper

Instructions

• In a large bowl, add the chickpeas, bell pepper, parsley, red onion, and celery.

• In a small bowl, whisk together the olive oil, lemon juice and garlic, and season to taste with the kosher salt and freshly ground black pepper. Add the dressing to the chickpea mixture and toss to coat.

• Serve immediately or chill up to 4 days. Before serving, add more salt and pepper to taste.

Avocado Caprese Salad

Ingredients

• 2 cups fresh arugula

• 2-3 campari or cocktail style tomatoes sliced

• 1/2 avocado pitted and sliced

• 3 slices fresh mozzarella cheese

• fresh basil leaves

• 1 tablespoon extra virgin olive oil I prefer the fruitiest, lightest flavored

• 1 1/2 teaspoons balsamic vinegar

• generous pinch of sugar or dollop of honey

• kosher salt and freshly ground black pepper

Instructions

• Assemble the arugula, tomato, avocado slices and mozzarella in a serving bowl. Top with torn or slivered basil leaves. Whisk the extra virgin olive oil in a small bowl with the balsamic vinegar, sugar or honey and season with kosher salt and freshly ground black pepper to taste and pour over the salad. Toss to coat and serve.

Citrus Shrimp and Avocado Salad

This simple but totally flavorful shrimp salad makes the perfect meal-prep meal for lunch or dinner thanks to pan-seared citrus-flavored shrimp, creamy avocado, and the crunch of sliced almonds.

Servings 4 salads

Calories 374 kcal

Ingredients

• 1 pound medium Pan-Seared Citrus Shrimp (I use 31/40 shrimp)

• 8 cups greens (such as arugula, spinach, or spring mix)

• Fruity or lemon-flavored extra virgin olive oil

• Juice of 1/2 lemon or 1/2 orange

• 1 avocado , sliced or diced

• 1 shallot , minced

• 4 ounces sliced almonds , toasted

• Kosher salt and freshly ground black pepper

Instructions

• Prepare the recipe for the Pan-Seared Citrus Shrimp, or gently warm the leftover shrimp. Or, if you prefer, serve the shrimp chilled.

• Toss the shrimp with the salad greens in a large bowl.

• Lightly drizzle with olive oil, and if desired, some of the sauce remaining from the shrimp with a generous squeeze of citrus, and toss lightly to coat.

• Add the avocado, shallots and sliced almonds and then season with kosher salt and freshly ground black pepper and serve.

Recipe Notes

Use some of the citrus sauce from the shrimp as a double duty dressing.

Or, if you don't have enough sauce for the dressing, simply use a good extra virgin olive oil (I like the lemon flavored varieties) with an additional squeeze of citrus.

Couscous with Sun-Dried Tomato and Feta

This easy couscous recipe works well served warm or at room temperature.

Ingredients

• 1/3 cup shelled pine nuts

- 1 tablespoon olive oil

- 1/2 teaspoon kosher salt

- 1 1/2 cup couscous

- 1/3 cup sun-dried tomatoes in oil, drained and diced

- 1/3 cup crumbled feta cheese

- 1/4 cup chopped green onion

Instructions

- In a dry, non-stick fry pan over medium-high heat, toast the pine nuts, tossing often, until golden brown, about 3-4 minutes. Be sure to watch them closely as they can burn quickly once they get hot. Set aside.

- In a medium saucepan, bring 1 1/4 cup water to a boil. Stir in the couscous, olive oil and kosher salt, cover, and remove from the heat. Let stand for 5 minutes.

- Fluff the couscous with a fork and stir in the sun dried tomatoes, feta cheese, chopped green onion, and pine nuts. This dish can be served warm or at room temperature.

Ingredients

• 1 tablespoon olive oil divided

• 2 bunches Swiss chard center stems cut out and discarded and leaves coarsely chopped

• 2 cups low-sodium chicken broth or vegetable broth

• 2 medium shallots finely chopped (about 1/2 cup)6 medium garlic cloves, minced

• 15.5 ounce can garbanzo beans chickpeas, rinsed and drained

• 2 tablespoons freshly squeezed lemon juice

• Salt and freshly ground black pepper to taste

• 1/2 cup crumbled feta cheese optional

Instructions

• In a larges skillet, heat 1 tablespoon of the olive oil over medium-high heat. Add half of hte chard and cook, 1 to 2 minutes. When the first half has wilted, add the remaining chard. When all of the chard is wilted, add the chicken broth. Cover the skillet and cook the chard until tender, about 10 minutes. Drain the chard through a fine sieve (strainer) and set it aside.

• Wipe out the skillet and heat the remaining 1 tablespoon olive oil over medium-high heat. Add the shallots and garlic and cook, stirring, until they are softened, about 2 minutes. Add the chard and chickpeas and cook until heated through, 3 to 4 minutes. Drizzle the lemon juice over the mixture and season with salt and pepper, to taste. Sprinkle cheese on top just before serving, if desired.

Greek Salad with Avocado

A simple Greek salad dressing completes this easy and authentic Greek salad with the addition of creamy avocado for a simple salad side dish that goes with everything.

Ingredients

• 2 English cucumbers peeled in stripes and cut into 1/2 inch slices

• 1 1/2 pounds medium tomatoes I use cocktail tomatoes, stemmed and quartered

• 1/4 small red onion thinly sliced

- 1 1/2 cups kalamata olives pitted and halved

- 1/4 cup Italian flat leaf parsley chopped

- 2 avocados pitted and cut into chunks

- 1 cup feta cheese broken into large chunks

- 1/2 cup extra virgin olive oil

- 1/2 cup red wine vinegar

- 2 cloves garlic peeled and minced

- 1 tablespoon oregano

- 2 teaspoons sugar

- 1 teaspoon each of kosher salt and freshly ground black pepper

Instructions

- In a large serving bowl, combine the cucumbers, tomatoes, red onion, kalamata olives and parsley. Place the avocado in a small bowl and set aside.

- In a small canning jar, combine the olive oil, red wine vinegar, garlic, oregano, sugar and salt and pepper. Top with the lid and shake well until blended and emulsified. Season with more sugar and salt and pepper to taste.

• Pour 1 tablespoon of the dressing on the sliced avocado and gently mix to coat. Pour the rest of the dressing on the cucumber mixture and toss to coat. Add the avocado to the salad and top with chunks of feta cheese, and serve.

Recipe Notes

As the salad sits, the juices from the vegetables will release, adding to the amount of dressing. If you prefer, reserve some of the dressing and add only if needed for more moisture.

This Greek salad keeps in the refrigerator for 4-5 days.

Whole Wheat Greek Pasta Salad

Ingredients

• 1/2 pound whole wheat penne pasta

• 2 medium tomatoes chopped or cut into 1/8ths (about 1 cup)

• 1/3 cup roasted red and/or yellow bell pepper roughly chopped

• 2 tablespoons capers drained

• 1/4 cup sliced kalamata olives sliced in half

• 1/4 cup extra virgin olive oil

• 1 tablespoon balsamic vinegar

• 2 cloves of garlic minced or pressed

• 1/2 teaspoon oregano

• pinch of sugar

• kosher salt and freshly ground black pepper

• 1/2 cup basil slivered

• 1/4 cup feta cheese

Instructions

• Bring a medium saucepan of water to a boil, add a generous dose of kosher salt and the cook whole wheat penne pasta according to package directions or until al dente. Drain and set aside to cool.

• While the pasta is cooking, combine the extra virgin olive oil, balsamic vinegar, garlic, oregano, sugar, kosher salt and black pepper in a small mason jar or any container with a lid and shake well. Add the tomatoes, roasted bell peppers, capers and kalamata olives to a medium bowl and pour the dressing over the vegetables and let sit for 15 minutes for flavors to combine.

• Add to the pasta and basil slivers to the veggie blend and fold. Season with more kosher salt and black pepper to taste and garnish with crumbled feta cheese. Add more olive oil if the pasta seems dry. Serve and enjoy.

Tomato and Hearts of Palm Salad

This salad takes just 10 minutes with a sharp knife for a little slicing and chopping to pull together and is the perfect addition to any potluck barbecue.

Ingredients

• 3 cups cherry tomatoes sliced in half

• 1 15- ounce can hearts of palm drained and sliced into 1/4 inch rings

• 1/4 cup thinly sliced or shaved red onion

• 1/4 cup chopped Italian parsley

• 1/4 cup vegetable oil

• 1 1/2 tablespoon red vinegar

• 1 teaspoon sugar

• 1 teaspoon kosher salt

• 1/2 teaspoon freshly ground black pepper

Instructions

• Combine tomatoes, hearts of palm, red onion and parsley in a large bowl. In a small bowl, mix the vegetable oil, vinegar, sugar and salt and pepper until sugar is dissolved. Pour vinaigrette over tomato mixture and gently mix. Add more salt and pepper to taste. Serve at room temperature.

Quinoa Tabbouleh with Chickpeas Recipe

Ingredients

• 1 cup cooked quinoa

• 1 can chickpeas garbanzo beans, drained and rinsed

• 1/2 pound Persian cucumbers or 2 hothouse cucumbers if using hothouse, seed the cucumbers first, sliced

- 2 cups cherry tomatoes halved

- 1 cup finely chopped green onion white and green parts

- 1 cup chopped fresh Italian flat-leaf parsley leaves

- 1 cup chopped mint leaves

- 1/3 cup fresh squeezed lemon juice about 2 large lemons

- 1/3 cup extra virgin olive oil

- kosher salt and freshly ground black pepper

Instructions

- Place the cooked quinoa in a large bowl. Add the chickpeas, Persian cucumbers, cherry tomatoes, green onion, parsley and mint and toss. In a small bowl whisk the lemon juice with the olive oil and season with kosher salt and freshly ground black pepper. Pour over the ingredients in the large bowl and mix well. Season with more kosher salt and freshly ground pepper to taste. Serve immediately or put in the fridge for flavors to meld.

Italian Chicken Wrap

Most grocery store delis use unleavened lavash flatbread for their wraps, but the lavash is hard to find for us regular folk. Instead, I use an extra large tortilla for these wraps for the best success at rolling without tearing your wrap.

Servings 1 wrap sandwich

Ingredients

• 1 extra large tortilla flatbread or lavash bread

• 2 tablespoons DeLallo Roasted Pepper Bruschetta

• 5-6 slices cooked chicken breast about 3 ounces

• Handful of arugula or spinach

• 2 slices provolone cheese

• 3-4 thin slices of tomato

• 2 tablespoons DeLallo Artichoke Bruschetta

• 10 sliced kalamata or black olives

• Sliced red onion

• DeLallo Balsamic glaze

Instructions

• Lay the tortilla or flatbread on a flat surface. Starting on the edge closest to you, layer a stripe of red pepper bruschetta about 1/2 inch inside the outer edge. Place the chicken slightly overlapping the bruschetta, then add a strip of arugula, then the provolone cheese and the tomato. Top with the artichoke bruschetta then the olives and sliced red onion and drizzle lightly with the balsamic glaze.

• Starting from the edge closest to you, fold the portion of the tortilla with the red pepper and chicken into itself, and fold the outer edges of the sides inward, then continue to tightly roll and wrap the sandwich. Slice the wrap in half and server, or cut the halves into even portions to serve as pinwheels. Make the day before or refrigerate for 2-3 days.

The BEST Chicken Piccata

This easy chicken piccata recipe's lemon-caper sauce is an Italian classic that can be made in just 20 minutes, making it everyone's favorite dinner.

Ingredients

• 1 lemon

• 1 1/2 pounds boneless, skinless chicken breasts

• 1 teaspoon kosher salt

• 1 teaspoon freshly ground black pepper

• 1/3 cup all-purpose flour

• 3 tablespoons butter divided

• 2 tablespoons canola oil

• 1 cup chicken broth or white wine, or a combination of both

• 2 tablespoons capers drained and rinsed

Instructions

• Slice the lemon in half, juice one half, then cut the other half into 1/8" slices and set aside.

• Trim any excess fat from the chicken breasts and slice in half lengthwise to make two thin cutlets. Season both sides of the chicken breasts evenly with the kosher salt and freshly ground black pepper then dredge each breast in the flour, shaking off any excess.

• Heat 2 tablespoons butter with the canola oil in a large skillet over medium-high heat. Add 4 pieces of the chicken and cook for 2-3 minutes per side. Transfer to a platter or sheet pan and cover with foil. Continue with the remaining chicken.

• Reduce the heat to medium and add the chicken broth or wine (or 1/2 cup of both) the lemon juice, sliced lemons, and the capers, scraping up the browned bits on the pan and cook for 2-3 minutes.

• Stir in the remaining 1 tablespoon of butter until melted. Taste for seasoning and spoon the sauce over the chicken breasts. Serve with mashed potatoes or cauliflower, polenta, or noodles.

Chopped Grilled Vegetable Bowl with Farro and Fresh Coast Retreat

This vegetarian Mediterranean bowl is filled with grilled vegetables and farro, then topped with a garlic yogurt sauce, kalamata olives, feta and hummus.

Servings 2 bowls

Ingredients

- 1 cup dried farro

- 3 cups vegetable broth

- 1 portobello mushroom

- 1 red bell pepper seeded and quartered

- 8 ounces asparagus

- 1/2 red onion sliced

- 1 zucchini sliced

- 1 yellow squash sliced

- Olive oil

- Kosher salt and freshly ground black pepper

- 1 pint plain Greek yogurt

- 1 clove garlic pressed

- 2 tablespoons minced cucumber

- 1 tablespoon lemon juice

- 1 teaspoon chopped fresh mint

- 1 teaspoon chopped fresh dill

- Kosher salt

- Red bell pepper hummus

- 1/4 cup halved kalamata olives

- 1/8 cup feta cheese crumbles

Instructions

- Rinse the farro in a colander under cold water then place in a saucepan with the vegetable broth and bring to a boil. Reduce the heat to medium and cook for 30 minutes or until the broth has been absorbed by the farro, stirring occasionally.

- Meanwhile, preheat the grill to high. Drizzle the vegetables with olive oil and season with kosher salt and freshly ground black pepper. Grill the vegetables, flipping once, until tender and grill marks appear. Pull from the grill and set aside.

- In a small bowl, mix the yogurt, garlic, cucumber, lemon juice, fresh mint and dill together. Season with salt to taste.

• Chop the grilled vegetables into bite size pieces. Split the farro into two bowls and layer with the grilled vegetables, a scoop of hummus in each bowl, half of the kalamata olives and feta cheese. Drizzle with the garlic yogurt sauce and fresh dill or mint. Serve warm or at room temperature.

30 Minute Pork Scallopini With Lemons and Capers

Tart lemons and briny capers give this sauce its signature taste over lightly fried, boneless pork cutlets for an easy Italian dinner that's on the table in just 30 minutes.

Ingredients

• 4 thin boneless pork chops

• 8 fresh sage leaves

• 1/4 cup all-purpose flour

• kosher salt and freshly ground black pepper

• 4 tablespoons butter divided

• 1 tablespoon vegetable oil

• 1/2 cup white wine

- 1/4 cup capers

- 1 cup chicken stock

- 2 lemons juiced

- 1 lemon sliced thinly

- 2 tablespoons Italian flat leaf parsley chopped

Instructions

- Pound out the pork chops to 1/4 inch thickness. Press 2 sage leaves into one side of each each of the pork chops. Mix the flour, kosher salt and ground black pepper in a large, shallow bowl or plate. Add the pork chops to the flour, one at a time, and flour each pork chop, gently turning on each side so the sage leaves stay on the pork chop. Gently tap off the excess flour.

- Heat a large skillet on medium high. Melt 1 tablespoon of butter with 1/2 tablespoon of the oil. Place 2 of the pork chops in the skillet and cook for 3-5 minutes on each side, or until golden browned. Remove from the pan and set aside. Add 1 more tablespoon of butter and the remaining oil. Cook the remaining 2 pork chops and place with the other two cooked pork chops.

• Wipe out any burned or really crispy bits out of the pan. Melt 1 tablespoon of the butter in the pan over medium high heat. Add the wine and capers and cook until reduced by half. Add the chicken stock, lemon juice and a few lemon slices and bring to a boil then add the remaining tablespoon of butter and stir, cooking for 2-3 minutes or until sauce thickens slightly. Add the pork back to the pan and warm in the sauce. Garnish with chopped parsley.

Grilled Greek Chicken Kebabs

Boneless, skinless chicken breast marinated in the traditional Greek flavors of lemon, garlic and oregano then threaded on skewers with a few veggies makes these grilled chicken kebabs an easy and healthy weeknight dinner winner.

Ingredients

• 1 pound boneless skinless chicken breasts (about 2 large breasts)

• 1/3 cup plain Greek yogurt

• 1/4 cup olive oil

• 4 lemons juiced, plus zest from one of the lemons

• 4-5 cloves garlic pressed or minced

• 2 tablespoons dried oregano

• 1 teaspoon kosher salt

• 1/2 teaspoon freshly ground black pepper

• 1 red onion quartered into 1-inch pieces

• 1 small zucchini sliced into 1/4 inch coins

• 1 red bell pepper seeded and cut into 1-inch pieces

Instructions

• Slice the chicken breasts lengthwise into thirds, and then slice again into about 1-inch pieces. Place the chicken pieces in a freezer bag or bowl and set aside.

• Add the Greek yogurt and olive oil to a medium size bowl. Zest one of the lemons into the bowl then juice that lemon with the remaining three lemons and add to the bowl. Add the minced garlic, oregano, kosher salt and black pepper and stir. Pour half of the marinade into the freezer bag or the bowl with the chicken pieces and reserve the other half of the marinade for basting. Marinate the chicken for 30 minutes or up to 3 hours in the refrigerator.

• When ready to grill, prepare the grill by lightly oiling the grate with vegetable oil or cooking spray and set to medium high heat.

• If using wooden skewers, prepare them by soaking in water for 10 minutes. If using metal skewers, no prep is necessary.

• Thread the chicken on the skewers alternating with the red onion, zucchini and red bell pepper until you've reached the end of the skewer, ending with chicken. Repeat with the remaining skewers. Discard any of the remaining marinade that had the chicken in it.

• Grill the chicken, basting the kebabs with the reserved marinade and turning often so each side browns and has light grill marks, until cooked through, about 10-15 minutes or until the chicken juices run clear. Serve warm. Refrigerate leftovers for up to 3 days.

Shrimp Pasta with Roasted Red Peppers and Artichokes

The Mediterranean flavors of roasted red peppers, artichoke hearts, capers and feta cheese meld with just a touch of cream to make a sauce that lightly coats pasta of any type.

Ingredients

- 12 ounces farfalle pasta bow tie or other pasta

- 1 1/2 pounds fresh or frozen medium shrimp in shells

- 1/4 cup butter

- 3 cloves garlic minced

- 1 12- ounce jar roasted red bell peppers drained and chopped

- 1 cup canned artichoke hearts in water or brine quartered

- 1/2 cup dry white wine

- 3 tablespoons drained capers

- 1/2 cup whipping cream

- 1 teaspoon finely shredded lemon peel

- 2 tablespoons lemon juice

- 3/4 cup crumbled feta cheese 3 ounces

- 2 ounces toasted pine nuts

- 1/4 cup snipped fresh basil

Instructions

- In a Dutch oven cook pasta according to package directions; drain. Return pasta to hot Dutch oven; cover and keep warm. Meanwhile, thaw shrimp, if frozen. Peel and devein shrimp, leaving tails intact if desired. Rinse shrimp; pat dry with paper towels.

- In a 12-inch skillet heat butter over medium-high heat until melted. Add garlic; cook and stir for 1 minute. Add shrimp; cook and stir for 2 minutes. Add roasted re peppers, artichokes, wine, and capers.

- Bring to boiling; reduce heat. Simmer, uncovered, about 2 minutes or until shrimp are opaque, stirring occasionally. Stir in whipping cream, lemon peel, and lemon juice. Return to boiling; reduce heat. Boil gently, uncovered, for 1 minute more.

• Pour shrimp mixture over cooked pasta; toss gently to combine. Garnish with feta cheese, pine nuts and basil.

Grilled Lemon Chicken Skewers

Greek flavors inspire citrus infused chunks of chicken thanks to a tart marinade that keeps the chicken juicy with a lemony punch.

Ingredients

• 2 boneless chicken breasts

• 3 lemons

• 4 cloves garlic minced

• 1 tablespoon dried oregano

• 1/4 cup olive oil

• 1 teaspoon kosher salt

• 1/2 teaspoon freshly ground pepper

• 7-8 green onions

Instructions

• Slice the chicken breasts lengthwise into thirds, and then slice again into about 1-inch chunks. Place chicken chunks in a freezer bag and set aside.

• Zest one of the lemons and add to a medium size bowl. Juice that lemon plus one more, add to the lemon zest and then add the minced garlic and oregano and stir. Slowly drizzle in the olive oil and whisk to combine. Add kosher salt and pepper. Pour the marinade into the freezer bag with the chicken chunks and let marinade for 30 minutes or up to 3 hours in the refrigerator.

• When ready to grill, prepare the grill by lightly oiling the grate with vegetable oil or cooking spray and set to medium high heat.

• If using wooden skewers, prepare them by soaking in water for 10 minutes. If using metal skewers, no prep is necessary.

• Slice the remaining lemon in thin rounds and then slice the rounds in half. Trim the bottoms of the green onions off and cut into 1-inch lengths.

• Thread one piece of the chicken onto a skewer then two slices of green onion, and then another piece of chicken. Fold a slice of lemon in half and thread next to the chicken, grouping closely on the skewer. Add another piece of chicken, then green onions and repeat the pattern until you've reached the end of the skewer, ending with chicken. Discard any of the remaining marinade.

• Grill chicken, turning often so each side browns and has light grill marks, until cooked through, about 10-15 minutes or until chicken juices run clear.

Greek Turkey Burgers with Tzatziki Sauce

Turkey burgers made with the Greek flavors of garlic, oregano, spinach, sun-dried tomatoes and feta cheese are a healthful option for burger lovers everywhere.

Ingredients

For the Turkey Burgers:

• 1 pound ground turkey

• ½ cup fresh spinach leaves , chopped

• ⅓ cup sun-dried tomatoes , chopped

- 1/4 cup red onion , minced

- ¼ cup feta cheese , crumbled

- 2 cloves garlic , pressed or minced

- 1 egg , whisked

- 1 tablespoon olive oil

- 1 teaspoon dried oregano

- 1/2 teaspoon kosher salt

- 1/2 teaspoon freshly ground black pepper

- 4 soft whole-wheat hamburger buns

- Bibb lettuce leaves

- Sliced red onion

For the Tzatziki Sauce:

- ½ cucumber , halved with skin and seeds removed

- 3/4 cup low-fat plain Greek yogurt

- 2 cloves garlic , pressed or minced

• 1 tablespoon red wine vinegar

• 1 tablespoon fresh dill , minced

• Pinch of kosher salt and freshly ground black pepper

Instructions

• In a large bowl, add the ground turkey, spinach, sun-dried tomatoes, red onion and feta. In a small bowl, whisk together the garlic, egg, olive oil and dried oregano and kosher salt and freshly ground black pepper then pour over the turkey and mix with your hands to combine.

• Divide the burger mixture into 4 portions and mold into patties. Place on a cutting board or plate dividing the patties with parchment paper and refrigerated for 30 minutes up to overnight. You could also individually freeze the patties at this point for up to 3 months.

• Prepare the tzatziki sauce by grating the cucumber. Gather the cucumber together and place in a paper towel and press the water out of the shredded cucumber and place in a medium size bowl. Add the yogurt, garlic, red wine vinegar, fresh dill, kosher salt and freshly ground black pepper and mix well. Cover and refrigerate for 30 minutes or up to 3 days.

• Heat a non-stick grill pan over medium heat and spray well with cooking spray.

• Place the turkey burgers on the grill, cover with an upside down sheet pan or lid and cook for about 5 minutes per side. Be sure to watch the burgers and monitor your heat as the burgers will brown quickly if the heat is too high.

• Slather buns with tzatziki sauce and garnish with lettuce leaves and red onion. Or serve bunless in the bibb lettuce leaves.

Saucy Greek Baked Shrimp

I made this baked shrimp recipe as a simple skillet dinner but if you'd prefer to serve it at the table, simply transfer it to a baking dish suitable to serve at the table rather than using the skillet.

Ingredients

• 1 pound large peeled and deveined shrimp (I like the Key West Pinks)

- 1/2 teaspoon red pepper flakes

- 1/4 teaspoon kosher salt

- 3 tablespoons olive oil

- 1 medium onion chopped

- 3 garlic cloves pressed or minced

- 1 15- ounce can crushed tomatoes

- 1/2 teaspoon ground allspice

- 1/2 teaspoon ground cinnamon

- 1/2 cup crumbled feta cheese

- 2 tablespoons chopped fresh dill

Instructions

- Preheat the oven to 375°F.

- Rinse and pat the shrimp dry and place in a bowl. Season with the red pepper flakes and kosher salt and set aside.

- Drizzle the olive oil in a heavy skillet and heat over medium heat. Add the onion and garlic and cook until softened, about 5 minutes. Stir in the spices and cook for about 30 seconds. Add the tomatoes and simmer, uncovered, for about 20 minutes, stirring occasionally.

• Remove from the heat and place the shrimp into the tomato sauce and crumble the feta cheese over the top. Bake for 15-18 minutes or until the shrimp are cooked through.

• Sprinkle with the dill and serve with crusty bread for dipping up the awesomesauce.

Slow Cooker Chicken Cacciatore

Slow-cooked bone-in, skinless chicken thighs create the luxe flavor in this savory Italian chicken dinner that pairs perfectly with pasta for an incredibly easy weeknight or weekend meal.

Ingredients

• 10 bone-in skinless chicken thighs , about 5 ounces each, trimmed

• Kosher salt and freshly ground black pepper

• Cooking spray or extra virgin olive oil

• 5 garlic cloves finely chopped or pressed

• 1/2 large yellow onion chopped

• 1 28- ounce can crushed tomatoes

• 1/2 medium green bell pepper chopped

• 1/2 medium red bell pepper chopped

• 8 ounces sliced shiitake mushrooms

• 2 sprigs fresh thyme

• 2 bay leaves

• Fresh parsley for garnish

• Grated Parmesan cheese

Instructions

• Generously season the chicken with the salt and pepper. Heat a large nonstick skillet over medium-high heat. Coat with cooking spray or a drizzle of olive oil and then add the chicken. Cook until nicely browned, about 3-4 minutes per side. Transfer to a slow cooker.

• Reduce the heat under the skillet to medium and coat with more cooking spray or another drizzle of olive oil. Add the garlic and onion and cook until soft, about 3-4 minutes, stirring occasionally. Transfer to the slow cooker.

• Add the tomatoes, bell peppers, mushrooms, thyme and bay leaves to the slow cooker. Stir to combine.

• Cover and cook on high for 4 hours or on low for 8 hours.

• Discard the bay leaf and transfer the chicken to a large plate or cutting board. Pull the chicken meat from the bones (discard the bones), shred the meat and return it to the sauce. Stir in the parsley. Serve with pasta, polenta or spaghetti squash topped with Parmesan cheese.

Healthy Greek Yogurt Tzatziki Sauce

This easy to make 5-ingredient Greek yogurt tzatziki sauce recipe is not only great with grilled meats, fish and gyro sandwiches, but makes a terrific, healthy dip for vegetables of every color.

Ingredients

• ½ cucumber , halved with skin and seeds removed

• 3/4 cup Dannon Greek Plain Nonfat Yogurt

• 2 cloves garlic , pressed or minced

• 1 tablespoon red wine vinegar

• 1 tablespoon fresh dill , minced

• Pinch of kosher salt and freshly ground black pepper

Instructions

• Prepare the tzatziki sauce by grating the cucumber. Gather the cucumber together and place in a paper towel and press the water out of the shredded cucumber and place in a medium size bowl.

• Add the yogurt, garlic, red wine vinegar, fresh dill, kosher salt and freshly ground black pepper and mix well

• Cover and refrigerate for 30 minutes or up to 3 days.

Mediterranean Quinoa Salad

This healthy vegetarian quinoa salad makes for a simple lunch or dinner, thanks to staples like roasted red bell peppers, kalamata olives, and feta from your fridge and pantry.

Ingredients

• 1 1/2 cups dry quinoa

• 1/2 teaspoon kosher salt

• 1/2 cup extra virgin olive oil

• 1 tablespoon balsamic vinegar

• 2 garlic cloves pressed

• 1/2 teaspoon dry basil minced

• 1/2 teaspoon dried thyme crushed between your fingers

• kosher salt and freshly ground black pepper

• 3 cups arugula

• 1 15 ounce can garbanzo beans drained

• 1 package DeLallo Zesty Salad Savors

Instructions

• Cook the quinoa according to package directions with 1/2 teaspoon salt added to the water. Cool completely.

• Mix together the olive oil, balsamic vinegar, pressed garlic, basil and thyme. Whisk until well combined. Season with kosher salt and freshly ground black pepper and set aside.

• To a large serving bowl, add the quinoa, arugula, garbanzo beans, and contents of the Salad Savors package (red bell pepper, kalamata olives and feta cheese).

• Drizzle with the dressing and garnish with basil. Season to taste. Serve at room temperature.

Recipe Notes

*Instead of a packet of Zesty Salad Savors, you can use the following instead:

• Small jar roasted red bell peppers (drained and chopped)

• 1/4 cup kalamata olives (roughly chopped)

• 1/4 cup crumbled feta cheese

Pesto and Garlic Shrimp Bruschetta Recipe

Garlicky shrimp top a simple bruschetta topped with pesto, sun-dried tomatoes, capers, feta cheese and topped with a balsamic glaze make this a simple but elegant appetizer.

Servings 12 -16 crostini

Ingredients

• 8 ounces 51/60 raw shrimp shell-on, fresh or defrosted

• kosher salt and freshly ground black pepper

• 4 tablespoons extra virgin olive oil divided

• 2 tablespoons butter

• 4 cloves garlic minced or pressed

• 1 french bread or sourdough baguette

• 3 ounces DeLallo Simply Pesto about 10-12 teaspoons

• 3 ounces DeLallo sun-dried tomatoes in oil slivered (about 1/3 cup)

• 2 ounces DeLallo capers drained (about 1 1/2 tablespoons)

• 1 ounce feta cheese crumbled

• 15-20 small fresh basil leaves, or 4-5 large leaves slivered

• Delallo Glaze Balsamic Modenacrem for drizzling

Instructions

• Remove the shells and tails from the shrimp and place in a bowl. Season with kosher salt and freshly ground black pepper. In a sauté pan over medium heat, add 2 tablespoons of the olive oil and 2 tablespoons butter and cook until melted. Add the garlic and cook for 1 minute until it becomes fragrant. Add the shrimp and cook slowly, flipping once, about 4 minutes or just until cooked through. Turn off the heat and let the shrimp sit in the garlic oil.

• Slice the bread into 1/4- to 1/2-inch slices. Place on a baking sheet and brush with the remaining olive oil and toast in the oven until golden brown.

• Slather each slice of bread with 1 generous teaspoon of pesto sauce, then top with a sprinkle of sun-dried tomatoes, 2 garlicky shrimp with sauce, capers, feta cheese and basil leaves. Drizzle with balsamic glaze and serve.

Pan-Seared Citrus Shrimp Recipe

This simple, bright, and fresh shrimp recipe is ready in under 30 minutes, making it an easy dinner for anyone on the go or the perfect appetizer to take to a party.

Ingredients

• 1 tablespoon olive oil

• 1 cup fresh orange juice (about 2 oranges)

• 1/2 cup fresh lemon juice (about 3 lemons)

• 5 garlic cloves , minced or pressed

• 1 tablespoon finely chopped red onion (or shallot)

• 1 tablespoon chopped fresh parsley

• Pinch red pepper flakes

• Freshly ground black pepper and kosher salt

• 3 pounds medium shrimp , peeled and deveined

• 1 medium orange , cut into wedges or slices

• 1 medium lemon , cut into wedges

Instructions

• In a medium bowl, whisk together the olive oil, orange juice, lemon juice, garlic, onion, 2 teaspoons of the parsley, and pinch of red pepper flakes. Pour the mixture into a large skillet set over medium heat. Bring to a simmer and cook until reduced by half, about 5 to 8 minutes.

• Add the shrimp, season with kosher salt and freshly ground black pepper, cover, and cook until they turn pink, about 5 minutes.

• Top with the remaining parsley and serve with orange and lemon slices on the side.

Recipe Notes

Fresh Gulf shrimp is a luxury for some of us landlocked folks, so I use frozen shrimp here instead. But if you can find fresh gulf shrimp, especially the sweet Key West Pinks of Florida, definitely go that route instead.

*Note that you can add the orange and lemon slices to the sauce to cook and brown slightly if desired.

Spicy Roasted Red Pepper Hummus

Ingredients

• 1 15- ounce can garbanzo beans rinsed and drained

• 2 tablespoons tahini

- 1/4 cup extra virgin olive oil

- juice of 1 lemon

- 2 cloves garlic chopped

- 2-3 roasted red bell peppers jarred or fresh

- 1 teaspoon chopped chipotle pepper in adobo sauce optional

- pinch of cayenne pepper

- pinch of kosher salt

Instructions

- Combine the garbanzo beans and tahini in the bowl of a food processor and process for 3-4 minutes or until super smooth. Add the extra virgin olive oil, lemon juice and garlic red bell peppers, chipotle pepper in adobo sauce, pinch of cayenne pepper and a pinch of kosher salt. Process for 1-2 more minutes or until smooth. Be sure to scrape the bottom of the processor and the sides so that all ingredients are well combined.

• Add more kosher salt and cayenne pepper to taste. If the hummus is too thick, add more olive oil 1 teaspoon at a time.

Greek Orzo Salad Recipe

INGREDIENTS

• 8 ounces orzo pasta (1 1/4 cup dry)

• 1 cup canned chickpeas, drained and rinsed

• 1/2 lemon, juice and zest (about 2 tablespoons juice)

• 1/4 cup minced shallot or red onion

• 1/2 English cucumber (2 cups diced, or substitute a peeled standard cucumber)

• 2 roasted red peppers from a jar or 1/2 fresh red bell pepper (1/2 cup diced)

• 1/3 cup chopped dill, plus more for garnish

• 1/3 cup chopped mint

• 2 tablespoons white wine vinegar

• 3 tablespoons extra-virgin olive oil

• 1/2 teaspoon Dijon mustard

• 1 teaspoon dried oregano

• 1/2 cup feta cheese crumbles

• 1/3 cup Kalamata olives, halved

• Black pepper

INSTRUCTIONS

• Prepare the orzo according to the package instructions. Taste the orzo a few minutes before completion to ensure it's 'al dente' (chewy, but with a little firmness in the center). When it's done, drain it and then rinse it under cold water until it comes to room temperature.

• Place the chickpeas in a bowl with the lemon zest, lemon juice, and 1/4 teaspoon kosher salt.

• Mince the red onion, then place it in a bowl with water (this helps to remove the sharp onion taste). Dice the cucumber. Dice the roasted red pepper. Chop the herbs.

• Stir together the orzo, chickpeas and bowl of lemon juice, red onion, cucumber, red pepper, dill, mint, white wine vinegar, olive oil, Dijon mustard, oregano, feta crumbles, black olives, and several grinds of black pepper. Taste and if necessary, season with more kosher salt.